Thread and Twine

By
Kilayla Pilon

Published by The Elite Lizzard Publishing Company 2023

In your eyes I do remember

Days of magnificent, handsome splendor

With great laughter and sorrow not known

Perhaps it is our hearts that have simply grown

And while my heartbeat echoes yours

Separate we must, in your eyes I remember

For I watch as you turn away, footsteps gentle as they carried you away

And as much as I feel like I've been strapped to a mast

Vastly surrounded by sea

Simply lost in who I may be

In your eyes I remember

Please don't forget me

Smears of cement so thick and heavy
Entrapment as it pours upon my feet
A travesty
Keeping me in fallacy
Of what freedom I wish upon me
I cannot step from this hardened prison
I am confined and my heart, my mind
- it's soon to flat line
And you, successful
Will survive my sorrowful malady
This cement you poured
Has swallowed my fire

In this water, a gentle blue
A soft wind blowing, the calm passing through
See not the cascading shadow above while seeking new
and effervescent love
Watch how to make your blood willfully flow
Your veins, spewing free
Know that the love is through
The bitter stab of cruelty, true

When I was young I was volatile

I didn't know left from right

And up or down seemed impossibly strange

I knew the touch of a cold sharp metal

Knew the cheerful pain of swallowing pills until I lay almost comatose

I didn't feel happy

I didn't feel sad

Hell, I wasn't even mad

I was trapped in a broken empathy

Where not a single person could stop me

So, I wielded my metal weapon

So small and dangerous in my hand

Because I didn't know any better

In this crazy fantasy land

Shattered wounds, alabaster scars, I'm caged
A scrapped metal collection of contraband
Bloodied tissue, blood shot eyes
All I say and all I ask
Please do not advise
I have no fight left

I hear the beckoning sirens call
Coming from the silver blade
It was my muse
My scarlet downfall
And while the scars have come to fade
The memories will forever remain
The days the blade kissed my skin
And fed the monster deep within

Left out of sight

You lurk in the corners of my panicked, frantic mind

Waiting, haunting, ready for a cruel embrace

And I am lost to this cruel rage

An enemy, a victim

While also partially a dinner

Perhaps I am nothing more

Then a passing, weak whisper

Who I am entrapped in this cage
A collection of cracked ribs
Bruises battering my heart
My soul a wisp of forgotten parts
Alabaster cavern, blood dripping from the stones.
I don't know how to free myself
From these catalytic emotions
Perhaps I am doomed to be confined
Inside this dark, lonely space in time

Tired eyes with exhausted circles,
A broken grin, a weak smile
I knew one day it would come
I, the wearied pilot, the crew of lonely few
It was that I knew would come
To wash upon the cragged bay, the rocks against the hull
Just as your touch tore my heart
The crash of the boat led me
To be melt into the sea, less failure be the only way

Lines of artistic sorrow, the water low within the porcelain home
Dripping to the linoleum floor
Oh, this is nothing new
For with a silver precious tool, the blood released anew
Perhaps one day I'll be one of the lucky few
For my words they came forth
A bubbling brook of sorrows station
Remember the artistic design, I have fallen into the pit of annihilation

Rivers run on sorrowed tears
Forgotten following of the fears
Traveling past the bubbling bank
Unforgotten, my heart sank
Like a sorted river run
Or a fool in the glum
This darkness that besets the rolling
Gently passing waves whilst falling
My tears have kept the river near
For I live here, buried in fear

If I were to lie my head
Close my eyes to this sense of dread
Perhaps this night would be my last
I found myself hoping fast
For mortality, it is a word
That shakes the mightiest of the herd
Yet for someone such as me
It breaks me free from malady

I cannot hear nor can I see
These monstrous words that torment me
In the shadows lay in wait
Vicious tones and berserk fate
Ears open to the sound
Yet wishing I could not be found
They lurk with mismatched toothy grin
Perhaps a sign I am a child of sin
One day their breath will fall on my flesh
Devour my once gentle soul, fresh
Their hunger and wait finally sated
While torn apart, I am obliviated

I do not know this beginning rule
Where a breath starts a story,
Yet I do not know what the middle holds
Shivering hands that scribble notes
Panicked breaths catching in my throat
This middle I do not know
The end is the only place to go
Chaos caused by my trembling hands
I do not know this beginning rule
And I don't believe I'm ready for the throw

A gasping breath that comes from me
Deep, profound, hiding profanity
I walk the streets of blue and green
The ocean open, where I am free
For to the gasping laughter fed to me
The idea of love, the idea of we
And while we dance beneath the moon
I understand, perhaps
I am one of the forgotten few

Lava spewed in touching emotion
My pounding heart a volcano,
A sorrow filled motion
For every yard of skin it touches,
Leaves another scar, another sinful motion
For I am rage and I am tears
Mixed emotions, childish fears
This bloodied lava pulsing free
I'd move on forever to forget
Me

Sorrows ocean waves
Come onto the gentle shore
Hungered water searching true
Knowing my heart, it belongs to you
These tides that pull to and fro
I'm sinking into the undertow
And my heart, shattered and thrown
I will drown in ocean waves
And at least then, perhaps
I will not be lost in the cavernous view

It yearned and ached
Like the hunger of a flame
Oxygen, a waste
A chemical saving face
But I was to lay into the fire
Consumed my flesh
A burning desire
For pain is all I've ever known
Perhaps desire and joy
Is something forever shown
That I will never find in this chaotic home

I sit in four walls
They make up a place called home
Yet silent these walls are
If they could whisper the truths
The sorrow of blood-stained bed sheets
And bruises given too
These painted walls may hold no scars
But within, they hold stories of great sin
And as such these very walls
I find them to be my friends
For both of us hold secrets
And live together again

It is with a sadness

A macabre sort of view

Where I speak through blinded eyesight

To wish through and through

That make some day the ocean current

Will pull me deep within

And together our hearts will join each other

I won't be so alone

Again

I loved as a rose
Thorny, protective, beautiful in prose
With red colours, oh so beautiful
But now I am wilting, am I?
My life, how it beats in my slowing heart
I will never forget that love we shared
And I leave this life, no longer full of beauty
Instead, wilted sorrow
Please, never forget me

In my eyes you always see
Pieces of a brewing malady
Sorrow boiling over the sides
Catalytic breathing, I'm lost somewhere in my mind
Where this water swallows me whole
And you, once so much a part of me
Sit and watch in your patient role
Letting me drown
And sink so deep below

Wounds gaping, holding multicolored words
Stories of valiant effort, survival the key hope
That every drop of crimson that slides down my skin
Is a triumph over a formidable foe
And I find myself wishing I could bleed something more
Perhaps an artistic blue
Or a pink, gentle hue
All I know is this pain
The way his hands have burned scars into my flesh
It is inescapable
I'll never forget the rotting of my heart
So instead, I take this rain of sorrow and sin
And paint me with crimson
Over and over again
While my heart beats against the cracks
And bleeds its last bit of hope

My arms, how they still feel each cue
Of bloodied blades and memories of you
Hands soiling my innocent flesh
The scent of alcohol on your heavy breath
My weapon I wield at a later day
To carve away the feeling of your skin
Bleed away the memory of your sin
I cannot forget, I cannot remain
Once a victim, reminded again
I one day wish to be free
But perhaps to do so I need to be free
Of me

Four white walls and dangerous views
Of splattered hopes and dreams turned to nothing but a
broken sight
I sit in silence, sit in rue
Where I could never forget you
For four white walls have become my home
That have watched every single aspect
Of you
And while my heart beats and painted words upon the
page
My talents have been tossed aside, left askew
Because now when I breathe into the flame of hope
I'm reminded that perhaps it'd be better to succumb
Because this flame, how it dances
Once a mesmerizing perspective of bright orange and
lashing blue
Now flickers in a small sway, burning through
And I realize I am an empty husk, an abandoned shell
Now trapped in a cataclysmic view
Because I trusted you

Is it me the weather forecasts in the mirror

Cracked beyond repair, shattered pieces

A dagger of damage that lay on the floor

Bloodied talents that follow me forevermore

I turn the light off

I have no desire to see the sore

That is my broken constellation of hope

Where even a simple word can make me suffocate, as the wounds leave me broken

My talent washes down the drain

The crimson colours and pallet of pain

I am a forecasted fatality

Your eyes once sparkled as vibrant a faraway star
Your smile, how it felt to be there to see the tender
expression
How that was all I wanted, all I needed
But alas, you are come and gone
Buried underneath, your laughter no longer sings
And I am left with the sorrowed rings
Of echoing heart break, once again in
Sorrows ocean waves
Come onto the gentle shore
Hungered water searching true
Knowing my heart, it belongs to you
These tides that pull to and fro
I'm sinking into the undertow
And my heart, shattered and thrown
I will drown in ocean waves
And at least then, perhaps
I will not be lost in the cavernous view

Fruitless are my efforts

No smile meaningful

No laugh bountiful

Instead, I lay in a single spot

Watch the days go by as I rot

Alone for years, it seems

Perhaps I am a poison

I snake through veins

Strangle away any source of joy

Smothering in my own decay

It seems the hope is long gone

The paint brush on the canvas turned to discarded brushes

The words of a poem into a desperate failing

I'm so sorry for who I have become

Because I was not meant to be

The beloved one

Deep inside your vibrant eyes
A love that cannot be disguised
Yet in my heart
It feels so empty
Like every throbbing beat
Was never meant to be
This while I love through and through
I am terrified I will forget you
Or perhaps forget the moments true
When blue skies reign and I
With love so pure
Sit beside you in pure blessed fervor
I still see inside your eyes
A love that cannot be disguised
But perhaps it's best if I forget
Perhaps if you go on your way
No matter the love that blossoms so true
I can't decide any more than you

Heavy eyes, exhaustion in its purest form
Into the mirror I stare
Where every breath I see in my hitched shoulders
Each breath, every blink
It's all just too much, I think
There is no tired that I can explain
Except for the scattered words in vain
I wish so deeply in my soul
That for once my heavy eyes
See only the darkest of shades
And my lungs which breathe every weakest breath
Would remind me I'm not ready to die
Yet

These drastic efforts
Become buoyant mistakes
That keep me afloat
With this snow-covered plate
Where razor blades drag thin white lines
And with the curled dollar bill
It feels so much like home
Where the burn is so comforting
And the heart beating tremors
There is nothing, no other feeling
Then the damming mistake of my wander

Rivers flow on gentle tides
Yet the rivers it does create
Are so diverse
Of crimson flowing, dripping down
A metal weapon, there is no crown
This river of crimson
How it trickles so
Regret sinks into the pit of who I am
I see these wounds
So drastic, so fueled
My gentle tides
A loss of myself, a loss of who I was
And forever a loss
Of whom I could have been

A flickering flame of orange hue
Embers flaking, flying high
It holds a desperate, beautiful thing
Where I once felt hope and prideful sting
Alone I've become
Buried within
I am lost to the beating heart of who I was
My flickering hope dying once again
The gentle orange fades
I watch it disappear day by day
And I have given into this decay
Because there is nothing else that I can say

Like footprints in the fallen slow
Marked impressions into the white glow
I've left the traces of my passage
In raised pink welts and pained drastic lashes
And while these wounds have come to be
A secret, cruel part of me
Like footprints in the fallen snow
These splattered wounds are all I know

Silver metals grip my effervescent soul
Tearing it to sheds
Whole by whole of my skin
Where pink stripes carved, a permanent blemish
The wings of change bring me years of change
I no longer see the bloodied weapon
As part of my beating hearts plan
But my soul, so broken, so torn and lost
I will never feel the warmth of four walls
That keep me safe
Instead, I will see every step
A mistake
And these weapons of metal will forever be
An unforgettable part
Of me

Ablaze the metal touches my skin
The sizzle a plain almost comparable
To the echoing sorrow trapped within
For each burn a freedom
A new exposed pain
I will never be free from the flame
It will chase me again and again
Set me ablaze, allow me to burn higher
I am alone in this self-made pyre

In your laughter
Echoing across the vast sea of sorrow
I hear a joy, I hear free and beautiful love
Passed along from one to one
Like the cry of an eagle or the call of a dove
You speak your love so fervently
It makes my beating heart feel so less empty
And when I feel your hand in mine
The coolness of your skin
It brings me a sort of peace
Again

Clinking glasses echo through the room
Echoed laughter, childish boon
Tired eyes and vomit spewed
Silent rooms with liqueur spilled
The laughter empty, no one remains
Sinking slowly into despair
Drinking with nobody there
Alone with choking vomit
Joyful giggles that turn to tears
Alone is the drinker
Hook line and sinker
Just one more bottle
Just one more glass
Until one becomes
A pile of ash

I sit here in wonder of the silver blade
These open wounds, the sorrows they say
For there's no pain that beats my frantic heart
Leaves my lost in the navy dark night
Where stars are swallowed whole by the stinging pain
And loneliness is all that remains
So deep runs the pain that can only be released
By drastic measures of a silver blade to my wrist

I sit in wonder with my heart beating true

Curiosity of survival feeling lesser few

Exhausted by these fighting desires

Such desperate pain is all I acquire

From days of breathing while my throat closes through

Alone, I feel it, nobody seeing true

These thoughts of bleeding wounds

What else can I do

But breathe the moment through

And hope that this metal weapon I carry with risk

Does not become the reason I take my last breath

A solemn emotion of broken-hearted view
Where loneliness feels partially true
No smile, no laughs
No beautiful smiles true
Instead, I am alone
Lost in the pale sky, blue
Where each spoken word
A smile crawl through
The broken-hearted mess
That has left me alone
So far away from you

The music played so gently true
My memory a dancing, beautiful view
Where smiles echo and laughter rings
I remember all these glorious things
While deep inside I swallow my pride
Ignore the depressive, dragging crime
Where the memories of lighter fuel
And wielded metal weapons too
Were simply far and few between
Instead of dancing in my kindred mind
Again, and again

It sinks into my heart
This endless echoing sorrows
Where each breath is labored
And my heart it beats so unfavored
I wish for death, a sweet release
But to so, so is to say goodbye
To the long love people who keep me
Up here, floating sorrowful in soiled sheets and spilled
stained blood
And so, I look at this metal weapon
A different angle
A different leverage
I am tired be it so
That one more day is just too much more

There is beauty that I cannot see
Coming from deep inside of me
Where these sharp metal toys
Free me from melancholy and painful insanity
My wings, may I fly like a dove
Gentle movements
The coo of a song
But I lay on the ground
Rain drowning me slowly
I cannot escape this form of shadowed cruelty
Please, lay me to rest
For this is all I'm meant to be

In the mirror I see
A body that I cannot embrace
I am not a friend of this battle wearied skin
Or the bagged eyes of sorrowful misery
My body it hungers for love
But we are strangers
Unknown to one another
Perhaps if I spill the ink of my palpitating heart
I might catch glimpse of who I am meant to be
But for now, I am quite sorrowful
I am far from free

Sometimes I sit and I stare
I watch the world so different, in despair
Watching people laugh, walk and smile
When for me a grin can take a mile
Of what little energy I bare
I have accepted I am alone
Unnecessary, unwanted, beholden
To this crashing wave of sorrow and bile
I have few words
Perhaps even less thoughts
Because I am too exhausted
Where do I even start?

Withdrawn tears and childish fears
Sometimes I wonder the difference
Between here and there
Perhaps the difference
In how each step takes me
It carries me forward
But my mind, pacified
Stays far behind
And I am alone
Cast aside, by a flame of hope I once held
Once nursed with gentle care
By allowing the tears of holding
The child who lived within me
But this flame has dwindled
Barely a smoldering ember
And I withdraw myself in fear
That my tears may smother the orange glow
With my childish fears

It is in my exhausted heartbeat
Where I sit and listen to the whistle of the wind
Where desperate hopes for foreign saving graces
I do not recognize the joy
I do not recognize the laughter
I am lost, tossed into a spiral of disaster
Hoping that every frantic breath
Keeps me closer, to feel alive
Then steps from almighty death
Alone is all I know,
Alone is all I see
And I suppose my frantic heartbeat
Is just a part of me
Like the scars that riddle my body
Where blood once pumped free
Where bones become enraged with infection
While veins echo a laughter of crimson
I will forever fight for this heartbeat
And sink into a bloodied scarring retreat

Peel my skin away from me
Free my flesh from the haunting touch
Where hands defiled
And scars grew wild
From white lines to pink welts
To raging infections, and heartbreak felt
A small silver weapons
Leaves me in the desert
Where the winds cause my lonely soul
To play in a pool
Of crimson cruel
Peel my skin away from me
So thus, I will not feel
The hands upon my skin
Perhaps it's overkill
But I only know one way to feel
And scarlet droplets upon the white sand
Is the deepest sense of this reveal
And while the wind blows around me
I cannot forgive myself for freezing
And I now otherwise wish
For a tiny glimpse
Into a world of dying

I suppose I should apologize
For drastic rhymes
And skin pulled together
With thread and twine
Or staples going in a straight line
I should apologize
For cardiac monitors wailing off and on
The wail of an ambulance in drastic time
Perhaps I should apologize to myself
For the dragon chasing perseverance
In the bottom of a bottle of wine
Or the dismantled razors laying in a line
I've come so far and am no longer intertwined
With handfuls of pills and intravenous lines
I'd like to say I feel a sense of pride
Because that old friend of mine
Found in plunging needles and thin white lines
Is no longer who I am
When it took me away from who I was
So, take it in
One single breath
And I'll remember
I am so much better than this

About the Author

Author Kilayla Pilon lives in Canada. She is an adamant mental health advocate and enjoys any act of creativity. Along with being an author she is also an artist focusing on impressionism. Her love of poetry is expressed in her vibrant words. She is also a fiction author.

Thank you for reading. Please leave a review!